— THE —
TOMATO
COOKBOOK

BASIC INGREDIENTS

THE
TOMATO
COOKBOOK

MORE THAN SIXTY
EASY, IMAGINATIVE RECIPES

EDITED BY
NICOLA HILL

COURAGE
BOOKS
AN IMPRINT OF
RUNNING PRESS BOOK PUBLISHERS

Philadelphia · London

Canadian representatives:
General Publishing Co., Ltd.,
30 Lesmill Road, Don Mills, Ontario M3B 2T6.

10 9 8 7 6 5 4 3 2 1
Digit on the right indicates the number of this printing
Library of Congress Cataloguing in Publication Number 94-72596

ISBN 1-56138-493-3
Printed in Singapore

Acknowledgements
Commissioning Editor: Nicola Hill
Editors: Isobel Holland & Jo Lethaby
U.S. Consultant: Jenni Fleetwood
Art Editors: Meryl James & Sue Michniewicz
Production Controller: Sasha Judelson
Jacket Photographer: Nick Carman
Photographer: Alan Newnham
Home Economist: Jennie Shapter
Stylist: Jane McLeish
Illustrator: Roger Kent/Garden Studio
Varieties text written by Joy Larkcom

This edition published in the United States of America in 1995
by Courage Books
an imprint of Running Press Book Publishers
125 South Twenty-Second Street
Philadelphia, PA 19103-4399

Notes
Microwave methods are based on microwave ovens
with a High Power output of 800 watts.

All the jellies, jams and preserves should be processed in a boiling
water-bath canner according to the U.S.D.A. guidelines.

To skin tomatoes, make a small cross in the top of each tomato. Drop
them into a bowl of boiling water and leave for 2-3 minutes. Remove
with a slotted spoon and allow to cool. The skin should now come off
easily but if the tomatoes are slightly under-ripe they may need a little
longer in the boiling water before the skins can be easily removed.

CONTENTS

No two people agree on what constitutes a well-flavored tomato, but perhaps "tart sweetness" is as good a description as any. Some people prefer the acidic element, others the sweetness but it is the subtle balance of the two in one fruit which seems to create outstanding flavor. For the best tomatoes marry this with the texture of the flesh and juiciness. Most people love a "meaty" tomato and juiciness – as long as the juice is flavorsome and not just "watery." What cooks and the discerning public abhor is the "taste of nothing" characteristic of so many tomatoes.

Flavor is influenced by many factors, the variety being one of the most important. Unfortunately many of today's commercial varieties are bred to travel well or to stand up to mechanical harvesting; flavor has been a casualty.

Secondly, a crucial factor in retaining flavor is when the tomatoes are picked. Within reason, the longer the fruit is left on the vine the better, and the sooner it is eaten once ripe, the better the flavor. The home gardener has the edge every time, as commercial tomatoes are often picked when green, plunged into cold storage and later ripened in warming rooms. This process eliminates most of the flavor.

Flavor is also affected by how tomatoes are grown. Ironically, tomatoes taste better if the plants are to some degree maltreated – a little underwatered and a little underfed. (Bad gardeners can grow very tasty tomatoes!) Even within one variety, flavor can vary during the season, from truss to truss, with the temperature, with the quality of light, and whether they are grown indoors or out.

Most varieties taste best when the skin color is fully developed and the flesh is firm. Curiously, good flavor seems to be associated with some of the green-shouldered varieties, which never fully turn red.

Tomato Types and Their Uses

Apart from the standard round red tomato, there are several distinct types, some being better suited to one purpose than others. While most tomatoes are red-skinned when mature, yellow forms exist in almost all types. Less common however, are tomatoes with pink, orange, and near white skins, while a few rare types remain green-skinned even when mature.

*Varieties * = Available rarely in the U.S.*

BEEFSTEAK TYPE

Burpee's Big Boy
As its name implies, a very large beefsteak tomato, with fruits often well over 1 pound in weight. Introduced in the 1940s, it has always been noted for its productivity and good flavor. Individual fruits are bright red, very smooth, firm, well-shaped, with thick walls and meaty flesh. Multipurpose. A hybrid variety.

Dombello *
A large-sized beefsteak, with fruits averaging 6-9 ounces in weight. Fruits are very deep red at maturity, with some greenness on the shoulders. They are exceptionally meaty and juicy, having very little central core. Flavor is good. Multipurpose; they are excellent sliced and broiled.

Dona
A beefsteak tomato with slightly flattened, very glossy fruits, averaging 5-6 ounces each. Well-flavored, with an excellent acidity/sweetness ratio and good meaty texture. Excellent general purpose tomato; ideal for slicing

in salads and for using in sandwiches.

Golden Boy
Very large, well-flavored, nicely rounded, firm fleshy fruits, often 2-3 inches in diameter and weighing up to 1 pound each. Wonderful deep golden-orange skin color, making it an eye catching ingredient in salads. General purpose, high quality fruit.

Golden Boy

MARMANDE TYPE

Marmande/Supermarmande
The classic, misshapen, irregularly ribbed French tomato. "Supermarmande" is an improved form of the original "Marmande" type. Its outstanding flavor and texture more than compensate for its ugliness,

though plenty of sunshine is necessary to develop the full flavor. Large, firm fruits are recommended both for use raw in salads and for cooking.

Supermarmande

CHERRY TYPE

Gardener's Delight
Surely one of the most popular of modern tomatoes. Cherry-size, thin-skinned, bright red fruits with exceptionally sweet flavor. Juicy "bite size" fruits are about 1 inch in diameter. Best used fresh in salads, but can be frozen whole. Very vigorous, tall growing plants, notable for their healthiness and abundant cropping.

Sweet 100
Very similar to Gardener's Delight in fruit and habit,

though the shiny, bright red fruits are a little smaller. Nicely balanced flavor: whether you prefer Gardener's Delight or Sweet 100 is purely a question of personal taste.

Sweet 100

Sweet Million
A variety which may supercede Sweet 100 as a salad tomato. The sweet-flavored, medium-size "cherry" fruits weigh ½-¾ ounce each. Plants fruit over a long season and keep well after picking. A hybrid, noted for its disease resistance and for its productivity. One plant may produce over 500 fruit!

Sweet Chelsea *
Large cherry tomatoes, usually averaging 1¾ inches in diameter, and weighing ¾-1 ounce each. Good, exceptionally sweet

flavor. Essentially used fresh in salads. Becoming a popular gardeners' variety, as the plants have a wide range of disease resistance, and crop early and abundantly. The fruits have good resistance to splitting and cracking late in the season. Hybrid, medium height plant, but side branches will set fruit if left untrimmed.

Sweet Chelsea

Tumbler *
A British bred variety suited for cool climates. Well-flavored, smallish fruits about 1½ inches in diameter. Primarily a salad variety. A bush hybrid, ideally suited to growing in pots and hanging baskets as the side shoots cascade over the edges making it a really decorative plant.

Phyra *
A small-fruited gardeners' variety, notable for the technicolor effects of the grape-size fruits as they ripen, crowding the plant with green, yellow, orange and red fruit simultaneously. The tiny fruits are slightly pointed, with an acidic flavor. Because of this, they are recommended as a salad garnish. A bushy hybrid about 12 inches, suited to growing in containers. However, in favorable conditions this plant can become quite rampant and sprawling.

Sungold
The tomato everyone loves - the golden counterpart for Gardener's Delight. Cherry size, thin-skinned fruits with exceptionally high sugar content. This accounts for the very sweet flavor which has been described as "tropical" and "winey." Very vigorous, tall growing, heavily cropping, healthy plants, typical of modern hybrids. Suitable for growing indoors or out even in cool climates.

GOLDEN PEAR-SHAPED

Yellow Pear
Daintily waisted fruits, 1-2 inches long and generally about

1 inch in diameter "across the beam." Pretty in salads and very appealing to children. Reports on its flavor vary from "wonderful" to "slightly acid" and "lemony" to "charming, pleasant and mild" perhaps reflecting a wider response than most to growing conditions. Undeniably it can be bland. Ideally used in salads for its decorative qualities, but can be lightly cooked.

Yellow Pear

PASTE, CANNING TYPE

Roma VF/Roma
The classic, long, almost conical Italian tomato bred especially for canning. The heavy fleshy

Roma

fruits are almost seedless. Relatively lacking in flavor, but has excellent qualities for making soups, sauces, purées, pastes and juices, and also suitable for barbecuing. Vigorous, essentially bushy plant , but can be grown as an upright, given some support. Plants are very prolific in reasonable conditions.

Britain's Breakfast *
A British-bred tomato, with fairly cylindrical, boxy fruits with a little pixie point at the top. Dense flesh and small seed cavity, like Italian paste tomatoes, and suited for use in purées and soups and in cooked dishes. Especially recommended

for freezing. Has a distinct sweet flavor and is equally good as a sliced salad tomato. A variety that doesn't normally grow very tall. Individual trusses can produce so many fruits that thinning is necessary! Over 100 fruits have been known to grow on one truss.

San Marzano
The standard Neapolitan paste tomato, with long, blocky, deep red fruits characterized by a tiny "pinnacle" at the top end. The true San Marzano should be able to stand upright on its square shoulders. Fruits notable for their high proportion of solid flesh and very small seed cavity, so ideal for making pastes and purées as far less boiling is necessary than with juicier varieties. Recommended also for bottling, canning and drying. Mild flavor with satisfactory sweetness/acidity balance. Moderately vigorous plants.

STANDARD ROUND RED TOMATO

Shirley *
A commercial European variety, producing heavy crops of firm, round, medium-size fruits of about 2 inches in diameter.

Well-flavored, with a good sugar/acid balance. Suitable for salads and for cooking. A fairly compact hybrid, noted for its good disease resistance and early cropping, and recommended mainly for growing in cold

Shirley

and slightly heated green-houses in a cool climate.

Ailsa Craig *
An old British favorite with a devoted following. Nicely shaped, round, mid-red, high quality fruits with particularly fine flavor, described as essentially sweet with a touch of acid. However, many strains have been developed and some have a noticeably better flavor than others. Essentially a salad tomato for fresh use. Heavily

cropping plants, suitable for growing outside and in green-houses.

Pixie
Very popular, bright red, medium-sized tomato of 1¼ inch diameter. Fruits well flavored and meaty. Good general purpose tomato. A hybrid with a very compact bush habit, making it ideal for container growing. Notable for its earliness, hardiness, productivity and fast ripening fruit. The improved Pixie hybrid has excellent disease resistance.

Alicante *
An old established European

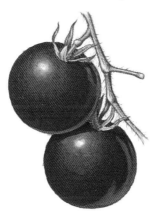

Alicante

variety, noted for medium-size, high quality, smooth, fairly sweet and well-flavored fruit. Acceptable for using either fresh or for cooking. Popular with gardeners because of its earliness, reliability, and versatility. Grown outdoors and under cover.

Counter *
A popular commercially grown European hybrid. Smooth, firm, round tomatoes with good texture. Flavor noticeably sweet but very pleasantly balanced with acidity. Quite fragrant. Used in salads and for cooking. Moderately tall with good disease resistance. Mainly a green-house variety.

Moneymaker *
A well-established European variety, producing uniform, round, red tomatoes, up to 2 inches in diameter. Very popular with amateur gardeners on account of its reliability. Its detractors say it is flavorless, but its advocates deny this. (The former are probably correct.) General purpose use.

Nepal
Introduced to the USA by a Johnny's Seeds customer and reputedly originating from

Nepal, the round, red fruits vary from moderate size in cool climates to near beefsteak size in good growing conditions. Flesh is firm and flavor outstanding. The flavor is retained even after plants are exposed to low end-of-season temperatures. Excellent in salads and for cooking.

Celebrity

An American hybrid, notable for its firm, well-flavored globe to slightly flattened fruits which average about 7 ounces in weight but can be much heavier. The tomatoes are rated highly for their color, texture, flavor and resistance to cracking. General purpose use. Very popular with gardeners on account of its vigor, disease resistance and general productivity. A bush variety – but it may benefit from some support to control its natural vigor.

STRIPED TOMATO

Tigerella*

Popular, round to plum shaped, medium-size tomatoes up to 2 inches in diameter. A pretty appearance as the skin is marked with red and orange stripes. Good, distinct flavor. Mainly used in salads for its

novelty appeal. Early ripening and heavy yielding. In Europe grown outdoors and under cover.

Tigerella

YELLOW TOMATOES

Golden Sunrise *

Round, smooth, very even, large fruits about 2 inches in diameter, notable for the yellow gold skin color. Normally a good, sweet flavor. Essentially a salad tomato but can be cooked. A variety which can be grown as a bush.

Golden Boy

A popular American tomato. Large, firm textured fruits, often weighing as much as 1 pound. Fruits are deep yellow orange both inside and out, with

notable flavor. Good for general purpose use.

Lemon Boy

An American introduction, notable for its "shocking yellow" skin color and lemony flesh. Fruits are smooth, deep globular in shape, and average 6-7 ounces in weight. The flavor is mild, but the fruits are very eye-catching in salads. An early cropping, high yielding hybrid, with good disease resistance.

Yellow Currant *

Bred by the British family seed firm, Robinsons, these tiny grape-size tomatoes are a

Yellow Currant

10

yellow orange when ripe. Thin-skinned, juicy, and mild-flavored, they are tailor made for use as a decorative salad garnish. Clusters can be picked whole. Rampant plants, which can be grown as cordons, or, if they are pruned especially hard, as bushes in large containers.

PINK TOMATOES

Ponderosa Pink
Popular American variety, with very large fruits, often weighing 1½ pounds each. Fruits are solid with firm, meaty flesh and small seed cavity. The skin color is an unusual purplish-pink. Very sweet, mild flavor; excellent if used sliced in salads and sand-wiches and can be cooked.

Oxheart Giant Oxheart/Grosso Gigante Cuor de Bue
An old Italian variety, produc-ing large, sometimes enormous heart-shaped tomatoes, often weighing well over 1 pound. Fruits are noted for their very thick walls and dense, solid flesh; they have little internal cavity and very few seeds. Their color is an attractive pink. Excellent flavor and texture. Good for use in salads and fillings for sandwiches, for grilling and cooking and

also for stuffing. A early cropping variety.

STORAGE TOMATO

Long Keeper
A unique tomato, originally sent to the American seed company Burpee by one of its customers, on account of its ability to store well for long periods after picking. The ripe fruits have an attractive gold-en orange skin color, with medium red flesh. They have a high acid content and a reasonable flavor, which is certainly superior to any out-of-season commercial tomatoes. For storage pick

Long Keeper

unblemished or partially ripe fruit before they have been touched by frost, and store ·indoors so they ripen naturally. They will usually keep from 6-12 weeks, and sometimes even longer.

Striped Cavern

STUFFING TOMATO

Striped Cavern *
Very boxy fruit, often 2 inches deep with exceptionally thick walls. The inside of this tomato can be scooped out to make a wonderful cavity for stuffing. Especially when immature, the skin appears lightly striped. An unexciting flavor: definitely for use as the messenger and not the message.

ITALIAN TOMATO SOUP

Serves 4-6

2 tablespoons olive oil
2 garlic cloves halved
1 onion, chopped
1½ pounds tomatoes, peeled,
seeded and chopped
4 cups beef stock
1 tablespoon tomato paste
2 tablespoons uncooked long-grain rice
1 tablespoon chopped fresh basil
salt and freshly ground black pepper
basil leaves, for garnish

Heat the oil in a large saucepan, add the garlic and sauté until golden brown. Remove and discard the garlic. Add the chopped onion and tomatoes to the garlic-flavored oil and sauté for 2-3 minutes, stirring frequently.

Add the beef stock, tomato paste, rice and chopped basil. Simmer over a low heat, for about 15 minutes. Season with salt and pepper to taste.

Transfer to a warmed soup tureen and garnish with basil leaves. Serve with freshly grated Parmesan cheese and French or garlic bread, if you like.

TOMATO & ZUCCHINI SOUP

Serves 4

3 tablespoons olive oil
1 garlic clove, crushed
2 pounds tomatoes, peeled,
seeded and chopped
2 tablespoons tomato paste
1 tablespoon chopped fresh basil
3 cups chicken stock
2 zucchini trimmed and coarsely shredded
salt and freshly ground black pepper

FOR GARNISH:

4 ice cubes
3 tablespoons plain yogurt
basil leaves

Heat the oil in a saucepan, add the garlic, tomatoes and tomato paste and cook over a gentle heat for 10 minutes. Stir in the basil and stock with seasoning to taste. Bring to a boil, lower the heat and simmer for 5 minutes. Purée the soup in a blender or food processor until fairly smooth. Leave to cool. Stir the zucchini into the soup; cover and chill for 4 hours, or overnight.

Just before serving, place an ice cube in each of four chilled bowls. Pour in the soup, add a swirl of yogurt and garnish with basil leaves.

Illustrated opposite

GAZPACHO

Serves 6

1 pound beefsteak tomatoes, peeled,
seeded and chopped
2 garlic cloves, chopped
3 tablespoons tomato paste
3 tablespoons olive oil
2 tablespoons red wine vinegar
2½ cups water
½ teaspoon sugar
1 cucumber, halved
salt and freshly ground black pepper

TO SERVE:

1 small onion, chopped,
or 6 scallions, chopped
croutons (*optional*)

Place the tomatoes in a blender or food processor with the garlic, tomato paste, olive oil, vinegar, water and ½ teaspoon sugar. Add salt and pepper to taste. Skin and coarsely chop one cucumber half and add to the processor. Blend at maximum speed for about 30 seconds, or until smooth. Stir in the remaining water. Refrigerate the soup for at least 2 hours.

Just before serving, dice the remaining cucumber and sprinkle it over the chilled soup with the chopped scallions and croutons, if using, or serve separately in small bowls.

Illustrated on pages 2-3

TOMATO & ROSEMARY SOUP

Serves 4

2 tablespoons olive oil
1 large onion, chopped
2 cups diced potatoes
3 cups chopped ripe tomatoes
grated rind and juice of ½ lemon
3 cups chicken or vegetable stock
2 rosemary sprigs
salt and freshly ground black pepper

Heat the oil in a pan. Add the onion and cook over moderate heat for 5 minutes, then add the potatoes and stir until well coated in oil. Cook gently for 5 minutes, stirring occasionally.

Add the tomatoes, lemon rind and juice, stock and rosemary sprigs, with salt and pepper to taste. Bring to a boil, lower the heat and simmer the soup for 15-20 minutes.

Purée the soup in a blender or food processor. Press through a strainer to remove the tomato seeds and rosemary. Return the soup to the clean pan, adjust the seasoning to taste and reheat. Serve in individual heated bowls.

MICROWAVE METHOD: Place oil and onion in a casserole dish. Cook on High for 2 minutes. Add potatoes, tomatoes, lemon, hot stock and rosemary. Cover and cook on High for 12 minutes. Purée and strain. Reheat on High for 2 minutes.

PEPPER & TOMATO SOUP

Serves 4

2 tablespoons corn oil
1 onion, finely chopped
2 sweet green peppers, cored, seeded and chopped
1 garlic clove, crushed
3 medium-size tomatoes, peeled, seeded and chopped
1 tablespoon tomato paste
3 cups vegetable stock
1 teaspoon dried basil
salt and freshly ground black pepper

FOR GARNISH:

2 tablespoons plain yogurt or sour cream
chopped fresh parsley

Heat the oil in a saucepan and sauté the onion until soft. Add the green peppers and cook for 2 minutes. Stir in the garlic, tomatoes, tomato paste, vegetable stock and basil, with salt and pepper to taste.

Bring the soup to a boil, cover and simmer for 30 minutes. Allow to cool slightly. Purée in a blender or food processor, or rub through a strainer. Return the soup to the rinsed pan and reheat gently. Pour into heated soup bowls. Swirl a little of the yogurt or sour cream into each bowl and garnish with chopped parsley.

TOMATO & CRAB SOUP

Serves 4-6

½ stick butter
2 onions, sliced
1 garlic clove, crushed
4 medium-size tomatoes, peeled, seeded and chopped
1 bouquet garni
⅔ cup dry white wine
3 cups fish stock
2 teaspoons grated lemon rind
2 cups cooked crabmeat
⅔ cup heavy cream
salt and freshly ground white pepper

Melt the butter in a large saucepan. Add the onions and garlic and cook over a moderate heat until softened. Add the tomatoes, bouquet garni, wine, stock and lemon rind with half the crabmeat. Stir in salt and pepper to taste. Bring to a boil, lower the heat, cover and simmer for 20 minutes.

Remove and discard the bouquet garni from the soup. Let cool slightly, then purée in a blender or food processor. Alternatively, press the soup through a fine strainer into the clean pan. Add the remaining crabmeat and stir in the cream. Reheat but do not boil. Serve the soup hot with crusty French bread.

CHERRY TOMATO CUPS

Makes 50

**50 cherry tomatoes, a mixture of
red and yellow**
**2 packages (*3 ounces each*) cream cheese,
softened**
a little milk
¾ cup smooth liver pâté
salt and freshly ground black pepper
parsley or dill sprigs, for garnish

Cut the tops off the tomatoes and slice small pieces off the bases, if necessary, so that they will stand level. Using a teaspoon, scoop out the seeds; sprinkle the insides with a little salt and pepper.

Put the cheese into a bowl and beat well until smooth, adding a little milk if needed to make a piping consistency. Using a pastry bag fitted with a shell tip, pipe the cheese into half the tomatoes; fill the remainder with pâté.

Garnish each tomato with a tiny sprig of parsley or dill, arrange on plates or trays and serve as appetizers or as part of a buffet.

BURGHUL & TOMATO SALAD

Serves 4

1 cup burghul (*cracked wheat*)
3 medium-size tomatoes, chopped
2 garlic cloves, crushed
2 onions, chopped
4 parsley sprigs, chopped
a few mint leaves, finely chopped
2 tablespoons chopped fresh mint

DRESSING:

3 tablespoons lemon juice
6 tablespoons olive oil
1 teaspoon salt
pinch of white pepper

Put the burghul in a bowl with water to cover. Soak for 45 minutes. Pour into a strainer lined with cheesecloth or a clean dish towel, drain and then squeeze the cloth to extract as much liquid as possible from the burghul. Tip the burghul into a bowl. Add the tomatoes, garlic, onions and herbs. Mix lightly.

To make the dressing, combine the lemon juice, olive oil, salt and white pepper in a screw-top jar. Close the lid tightly and shake well. Pour the dressing over the salad and toss lightly. Set aside for at least 30 minutes to allow the flavors to blend. Serve at room temperature.

Illustrated opposite

TOMATOES WITH HORSERADISH SAUCE

Serves 4

**1 pound yellow currant or
cherry tomatoes
6 tablespoons mayonnaise
2 tablespoons sour cream
2 tablespoons plain yogurt
2 teaspoons lemon juice
3 tablespoons horseradish sauce,
or 1-2 tablespoons grated horseradish
1½ tablespoons chopped fresh dill
1 dill sprig, for garnish**

Pile the tomatoes in a pyramid on a flat dish. In a bowl combine the mayonnaise with the sour cream and yogurt, then stir in the lemon juice, horseradish and dill.

Spoon the horseradish sauce over the tomatoes just before serving. Garnish with the dill sprig.

CASHEW & TOMATO SALAD

Serves 4

**2 crisp eating apples, peeled,
cored and coarsely chopped
2 teaspoons lemon juice
½ cup salted cashews, chopped
4 plum tomatoes, sliced
lettuce leaves, to serve
1 tablespoon chopped fresh dill, for garnish**

DRESSING:

**1 tablespoon white wine vinegar
2 tablespoons corn oil
1 garlic clove, crushed
1 teaspoon wholegrain mustard
¼ teaspoon sugar
¼ teaspoon freshly ground black pepper**

Put the chopped apples into a bowl and stir in the lemon juice, cashews and tomatoes.

To make the dressing, combine all the ingredients in a screw-top jar. Close the lid tightly and shake well. Add the dressing to the tomato mixture and toss gently to coat all the ingredients.

Serve the salad in a bowl lined with lettuce leaves and garnish with chopped dill.

GREEN TOMATO & PASTA SALAD

Serves 4-6

1 pound cooked pasta twists
2 pounds large green tomatoes
2 tablespoons olive oil
6 garlic cloves, thickly sliced
1 tablespoon white wine vinegar
salt and freshly ground black pepper

Bring a large saucepan of lightly salted water to a boil. Add the pasta twists and cook until just tender. Drain, rinse under cold water and drain again. Transfer to a salad bowl.

Dice the tomatoes, removing as much seed pulp as possible. Heat the oil in a large skillet, add the garlic and cook until golden. Stir in the tomatoes, cover the pan, and cook for 6-8 minutes over a low heat.

Stir the vinegar into the tomato mixture, with salt and pepper to taste. Add to the cooked pasta and toss lightly. Serve the salad cold or at room temperature.

TOMATOES WITH YOGURT & BASIL

Serves 4

1½ pounds tomatoes, peeled,
seeded and coarsely chopped
3 tablespoons butter
1 cup plain yogurt
2 teaspoons chopped fresh basil
¼ cup pignoli (*pine nuts*), toasted
salt and freshly ground black pepper
whole wheat toast triangles,
or slices of pita bread, for garnish

Drain away any excess juice from the tomatoes by leaving them on a sloping board or in a colander for 10 minutes.

Melt the butter in a skillet and cook the tomatoes gently for a few minutes, until just softened but not mushy. Remove the skillet from the heat. Add salt and pepper to taste.

Beat the yogurt in a bowl until smooth, then stir into the tomatoes. Stir in the chopped basil, pour into a shallow serving dish and scatter the pignoli over the top. Garnish with whole wheat toast triangles or with sliced pita bread.

Serve immediately, or keep warm for a short time, but do not attempt to reheat after adding the yogurt. This dish should be served warm rather than hot.

PIQUANT TOMATO SALAD

Serves 4

2 plum tomatoes, quartered
2 firm round tomatoes, quartered
8 cherry tomatoes, halved
1 celery stalk, sliced
1 red onion, thinly sliced
1 teaspoon cumin seeds
2 anchovy fillets, chopped

DRESSING:

4 teaspoons Dijon mustard
2 tablespoons white or red wine vinegar
6 tablespoons olive oil
salt and freshly ground black pepper

To make the dressing, place the mustard in a bowl and stir in the vinegar. Season lightly with salt and plenty of pepper and whisk in the olive oil until the mixture is well blended.

Place the tomatoes in a salad bowl with the celery, onion, cumin seeds and anchovy fillets. Add the dressing and toss until all the ingredients are well mixed. Serve at once.

Illustrated on front jacket

TOMATO & FETA CHEESE SALAD

Serves 4

¾ pound beefsteak tomatoes, thinly sliced
1 red onion, thinly sliced
2 teaspoons chopped fresh oregano
⅔ cup crumbled feta cheese
4-6 tablespoons olive oil
salt and freshly ground black pepper

Arrange the tomato and onion slices on a serving plate. Sprinkle with the chopped oregano. Add the crumbled feta, with salt and pepper to taste.

Spoon the olive oil evenly over the top of the salad. Let stand at room temperature for 20 minutes to allow the flavors to mingle. Serve immediately.

Illustrated opposite

MIXED BARBECUED VEGETABLES

Serves 6-8

2 red onions
2 sweet yellow peppers
2 sweet green peppers
1 large eggplant
about 1 cup olive oil
2 garlic cloves, crushed
2 tablespoons chopped fresh parsley
8 plum tomatoes, halved
3 firm zucchini halved lengthwise
12 large firm mushrooms, trimmed
salt and freshly ground black pepper

Remove the outer skin from the onions, leaving the point intact. Cut each onion in half horizontally. Trim the stem end of each pepper neatly. Cut the eggplant in half lengthwise. Score the flesh, without cutting through the skin and sprinkle generously with salt. Leave to drain upside down on a wire rack for 30 minutes.

Brush the cut surface of the onion with olive oil and place cut-side down on a barbecue rack over hot coals. Brush the peppers with olive oil and place on the barbecue grill; once the skin is charred, turn them over. Continue to turn the peppers until the skin is completely charred, eventually standing them upright. Transfer to a plate.

Once they have cooled enough to handle, peel the peppers and cut them into strips, discarding the seeds. Put the strips into a bowl and add ¼ cup of the olive oil with salt and pepper to taste. Stir in the garlic and the parsley. As soon as the cut surfaces of the onions are charred, turn them over, making sure that they do not collapse, and move them to the edge of the barbecue grill. When the onions are charred all over and tender, cut them into chunks, discarding any parts that are very black. Add the onion to the peppers, stirring in a little extra oil.

Rinse the eggplant halves and pat them dry with paper towels. Brush the cut surfaces with olive oil and place cut-side down on the barbecue grill. Cook for 10-15 minutes, turning once during cooking. (The eggplant is cooked when the center flesh is creamy and tender – it will become bitter if overcooked.) Meanwhile, brush the tomatoes, zucchini and mushrooms with olive oil and cook for 8-10 minutes, turning during cooking.

When the mushrooms, zucchini, tomatoes and eggplant are cooked, transfer them to a shallow serving dish, and serve with the cold onions and peppers.

CELERIAC & TOMATOES WITH LEMON SAUCE

Serves 4

1 tablespoon butter
1 celeriac, coarsely chopped
⅔ cup vegetable stock
¼ cup lemon juice
¾ pound tomatoes, cut into wedges
pinch of dried basil
1 egg yolk
2 tablespoons heavy cream
salt and freshly ground black pepper
basil sprigs, for garnish

Melt the butter in a large saucepan, add the celeriac and cook for 4-5 minutes. Add the stock and lemon juice and cook over a low heat for 5 minutes. Stir in the tomatoes and basil with salt and pepper to taste, taking care not to break up the tomatoes. Cook over a low heat, for about 7-10 minutes, or until the celeriac is tender.

Beat the egg yolk with the cream in a cup. Remove the vegetables from the heat and add the egg and cream mixture, stirring constantly. Transfer to a warmed serving dish, garnish with the basil and serve.

FRIED TOMATOES WITH CREAM

Serves 4

8 bacon slices
2-3 large green or very firm red tomatoes,
about ½ pound each
½ cup all-purpose flour
ground nutmeg
a little butter (*optional*)
¾ cup light cream
salt and freshly ground black pepper
chopped fresh parsley, for garnish

Gently sauté the bacon in a large skillet until crisp. Remove with a slotted spoon; leave to drain on paper towels. Cut each tomato into eight slices, ½-inch thick, discarding the stem end and base. Season the flour well with salt, pepper and nutmeg. Spread out on a plate, add tomato slices and coat on all sides.

Cook half the tomatoes in the rendered bacon fat over a moderately high heat until lightly browned. Turn once, adding a little butter if necessary to prevent sticking. Gently remove tomatoes and place on a serving plate; keep warm. Cook the remaining tomatoes.

Pour the cream into the skillet, bring to a boil, scraping the bottom to incorporate the brown bits. Pour sauce over the tomatoes and garnish with parsley. Arrange bacon slices in a criss-cross pattern on the tomatoes and serve.

ITALIAN STUFFED TOMATOES

Serves 4

8 large round or 4 marmande tomatoes
1 tablespoon corn oil
1 garlic clove, crushed
1 large onion, finely chopped
2 celery stalks, finely chopped
6 bacon slices, finely chopped
1½ cups cooked long-grain white rice
2 tablespoons whole kernel corn
1 teaspoon dried oregano or marjoram
2 tablespoons chopped fresh parsley
¼ cup grated Parmesan cheese
salt and freshly ground black pepper

Slice the tops off the tomatoes and reserve. Scoop out the insides and reserve. Heat the oil in a saucepan, add the garlic, onion, celery, bacon and tomato pulp and cook gently for about 5 minutes. Remove from the heat, mix in the rice, corn and herbs with salt and pepper to taste.

Fill tomatoes with bacon mixture, piling it up, and place in a lightly greased ovenproof dish. Sprinkle with Parmesan, replace tomato lids and cover. Bake in a preheated oven, 350°F, for about 20-25 minutes until the tomatoes are cooked. Uncover for the last 5 minutes. Serve hot or cold.

Illustrated on page 1

TOMATO & VEGETABLE KABOBS

Serves 2-4

2 zucchini, sliced
24 yellow or red cherry tomatoes,
or a mixture of both
1 onion, cut into 8 wedges
8 shiitake mushrooms

MARINADE:
1 tablespoon soy sauce
2 tablespoons olive oil
1 teaspoon wholegrain mustard
salt and freshly ground black pepper

Mix the marinade ingredients together. Bring a saucepan of water to a boil. Add the zucchini slices and blanch for 1 minute. Drain well.

Thread the cherry tomatoes, zucchini slices, onion wedges and mushrooms onto four long or eight short skewers and brush with the marinade. Leave the kabobs to marinate for 30 minutes. Cook under a preheated broiler or on a barbecue for about 5-10 minutes, turning from time to time. Serve immediately.

Illustrated opposite

SAUTEED CHERRY TOMATOES

Serves 4

½ stick butter or margarine
1 large onion, sliced into rings
1 teaspoon dried basil
1 pound cherry tomatoes
1 teaspoon sugar
salt and freshly ground black pepper
chopped fresh parsley, for garnish

Melt the butter or margarine in a skillet. Add the onion and basil and sauté until softened. Add the tomatoes and sprinkle with sugar, salt and pepper. Cook over a moderate heat, stirring gently, for 3-4 minutes or just until the skins begin to split.

Spoon into a serving dish and sprinkle with chopped parsley. Serve hot.

OKRA WITH TOMATOES

Serves 4

⅓ cup clarified butter or ½ stick butter
and 2 tablespoons corn oil
4 green cardamom pods, split open
1 small onion, thinly sliced
1 pound okra, trimmed and sliced in chunks
1 pound tomatoes, peeled and quartered
1 teaspoon garam masala
2 tablespoons chopped fresh cilantro leaves
salt and freshly ground black pepper

Melt the clarified butter or butter and oil in a pan. Add the cardamoms. Sauté for a few seconds, then add the onion and a little salt and pepper. Cook until soft but not browned.

Add the okra and tomatoes to the pan and cook for 8-10 minutes, stirring the vegetables frequently. The okra should be tender – avoid overcooking them or they will become slimy.

As soon as the vegetables are cooked, sprinkle on the garam masala and chopped cilantro. Serve immediately as a vegetable dish or as an accompaniment to curries.

MICROWAVE METHOD: Place butter and oil in a casserole dish. Cook on High for 30 seconds. Add cardamom and onion and cook on High for 3 minutes. Add okra and tomatoes, cover and cook on High for 7-8 minutes, stirring twice. Finish as above.

CAULIFLOWER & TOMATO SOUFFLE

Serves 4

½ cauliflower, divided into flowerets
3 tablespoons butter
½ cup fresh white bread crumbs
½ pound tomatoes, peeled and sliced
a few basil or tarragon leaves
¾ cup shredded sharp Cheddar cheese
¼ cup all-purpose flour
⅔ cup milk
3 eggs, separated
salt and freshly ground black pepper

Cook the cauliflower in salted boiling water until just tender. Drain, cool. Butter the inside of a 7-cup soufflé dish with 1 tablespoon of the butter, sprinkle dish with bread crumbs. Place cauliflower and tomatoes in dish, season, sprinkle with herbs and half the cheese.

Melt remaining butter in a small saucepan. Stir in the flour, cook for 30 seconds. Add milk gradually, stirring until the sauce boils and thickens. Remove from heat. When cool, beat the egg yolks and add to sauce with ¼ cup of the remaining cheese. Season to taste.

Whisk egg whites and fold into sauce. Pour over the vegetables. Sprinkle with remaining cheese. Bake in a preheated oven, 375°F, for 25-30 minutes or until risen and golden brown. Serve at once.

NUT-STUFFED TOMATOES

Serves 4

4 marmande tomatoes
salt

STUFFING:

3 tablespoons corn oil
1 cup minced mushrooms
1 cup cooked brown rice
½ cup coarsely chopped Brazil nuts
¼ cup currants
2 teaspoons chopped fresh basil,
or 1 teaspoon dried
freshly ground black pepper

FOR GARNISH:

⅓ cup sour cream
watercress sprigs

Cut the tomatoes in half, scoop out the pulp and discard. Sprinkle the shells with salt and place in a baking dish. To prepare the stuffing, heat the oil in a small pan and gently cook the mushrooms for 5 minutes. Stir in the cooked rice, nuts, dried currants and basil. Add a little salt and plenty of pepper. Spoon the stuffing into the tomato halves.

Cover the dish with foil and bake in a preheated oven, 350°F, for 25-30 minutes. Remove from the oven, top each stuffed tomato with a little sour cream and garnish with watercress. Serve piping hot.

ZUCCHINI NEAPOLITAN

Serves 4

1 tablespoon olive oil
1 small onion, chopped
1 garlic clove, chopped
1 pound tomatoes, peeled,
  seeded and chopped
1½ pounds zucchini, cut into ½-inch slices
2 tablespoons all-purpose flour
¼ stick butter
1¼ cups shredded mozzarella cheese
¼ cup grated Parmesan cheese
salt and freshly ground black pepper

Heat the olive oil in a small saucepan, add the onion and garlic and sauté over a moderate heat for 5 minutes. Stir in the tomatoes, with salt and pepper to taste. Bring to a boil, lower the heat and simmer for 10 minutes, to make a thick tomato sauce.

Cut the zucchini slices into halves or quarters, depending on size. Shake in a bag with the flour to coat evenly, and cook in the butter in a skillet until brown on both sides.

In a shallow baking dish, layer the zucchini then half the mozzarella, then the tomato mixture and the remaining mozzarella. Sprinkle over the Parmesan. Bake in a preheated oven, 375°F, for 30 minutes.

TOMATO, SPINACH & RICOTTA CASSEROLE

Serves 4-6

1½ pounds spinach, shredded
1 tablespoon water
¼ stick butter
1 onion, chopped
1 garlic clove, crushed
2 beefsteak tomatoes, peeled and sliced
1½ cups ricotta cheese
salt and freshly ground black pepper
2 tablespoons grated Parmesan cheese

Put the spinach in a saucepan with the water and a little salt. Cook for 2-3 minutes until soft, then drain well and place in a bowl.

Use a little of the butter to grease a casserole dish. Melt the remaining butter in a pan, add the onion and garlic and cook until soft. Stir into the spinach and mix well. Layer half the spinach, half the sliced tomatoes and half the ricotta in the casserole dish. Repeat the layers, seasoning each layer with salt and pepper. Sprinkle the Parmesan over the top.

Cover the casserole and bake in a preheated oven, 350°F, for 30 minutes. Remove lid and return to the oven for a further 10 minutes to brown the top.

Illustrated opposite

TOMATO-STUFFED EGGPLANT

Serves 2

1 eggplant
2 tablespoons olive oil
1 garlic clove, crushed
1 small onion, chopped
½ pound tomatoes, peeled and chopped
½-1 teaspoon dried oregano
2 tablespoons grated Parmesan cheese
1 tablespoon chopped fresh parsley
salt and freshly ground black pepper

Cut the eggplant in half lengthwise. Scoop out and reserve the inside, leaving ½ inch of flesh in the shell. Place the eggplant shells in an oiled baking dish and brush the insides with a little of the oil. Bake in a preheated oven, 350°F, for 15 minutes.

Meanwhile, chop the eggplant flesh finely. Heat the remaining oil in a skillet, add the garlic and onion, and cook for 5 minutes until softened. Add the eggplant flesh, tomatoes and oregano with salt and pepper to taste. Stir well and simmer for 10 minutes.

Divide the tomato mixture among the eggplant shells, sprinkle with Parmesan and parsley and return to the oven for a further 15-20 minutes. Serve hot or cold.

BAKED TOMATOES WITH GARLIC

Serves 6

¼ cup olive oil
6 plum tomatoes, halved
1 garlic clove, minced
3 tablespoons chopped fresh parsley
½ cup fresh bread crumbs
salt and freshly ground black pepper

Heat the olive oil in a large skillet. Add the tomatoes, cut-side down, and cook over a low heat for 6 minutes, turning them over after 4 minutes.

Place in an ovenproof dish and sprinkle with salt and pepper to taste, the garlic, parsley and bread crumbs. Drizzle with the oil remaining in the skillet. Bake in a preheated oven, 350°F, for 40 minutes.

RATATOUILLE

Serves 6-8

1 pound eggplant
1½ pounds large, firm ripe
tomatoes, peeled
½ cup olive oil
2 large red onions, sliced
2 sweet green peppers, cored, seeded
and cut into 1-inch squares
1 pound zucchini, trimmed
and cut into 1-inch slices
3 large garlic cloves, halved lengthwise
water or tomato juice (*see method*)
2 teaspoons sugar
salt and freshly ground black pepper

FOR GARNISH:

finely chopped fresh parsley
ripe pitted olives

Trim off the stem ends of the eggplant and discard. Cut the eggplant into 1-inch cubes. Toss in salt and leave in a colander for 30 minutes to extract the excess moisture.

Cut the tomatoes into chunks and scoop out the pulp and seeds into a strainer set over a liquid measure. Rinse the eggplant cubes under cold running water, drain and pat dry with paper towels.

Heat half the oil in a Dutch oven. Add the onions and simmer, stirring frequently, for 10 minutes, or until softened. Using a slotted spoon, transfer the onions to a bowl and set aside.

Add the green peppers to the oil remaining in the pan and soften them over a low heat for 5 minutes. Add them to the onions. Raise the heat to moderate, add the zucchini and sauté until golden. Add them to the other sautéed vegetables. Add the remaining oil to the pan. When hot, cook the eggplant cubes. Return all the vegetables to the Dutch oven together with the chopped tomatoes and the garlic.

Rub the strained tomato pulp through the strainer, adding water or tomato juice as needed to make ⅔ cup. Stir in the sugar, 1 tablespoon of salt and a generous grinding of black pepper. Pour the mixture over the vegetables. Stir lightly, cover and cook over a low heat for 30 minutes. Turn the vegetables over from top to bottom and cook, covered, for a further 15 minutes. Most of the cooking liquid should have evaporated. If not, remove the lid and cook for a further 5-10 minutes – the vegetables should be soft but not disintegrating.

Allow the ratatouille to cool slightly before adjusting the seasoning to taste. Serve it lukewarm or lightly chilled, garnished with the finely chopped parsley and ripe olives.

GREEN BEAN
& TOMATO
CASSEROLE

Serves 6

**1½ pounds green beans,
stemmed and heads removed**
1½ cups broccoli flowerets
½ pound mozzarella cheese
1 tablespoon butter or margarine
2 onions, sliced
1-2 garlic cloves, sliced
**1¼ pounds plum tomatoes, peeled,
seeded and chopped**
2 scallions, sliced
2 tablespoons grated Parmesan cheese
salt and freshly ground black pepper
a few fresh herb sprigs, for garnish (*optional*)

Bring a large saucepan of water to a boil, add the beans and broccoli flowerets and blanch for 3 minutes. Drain.

Meanwhile, shred 3 tablespoons of the mozzarella and thinly slice the remainder. Set aside.

Melt the butter or margarine in a saucepan, add the sliced onions and garlic and cook gently for 5 minutes until soft. Stir in the chopped tomatoes, bring to a boil and cook, uncovered, for 15 minutes until thickened. Stir in the sliced scallions and season to taste with salt and pepper, then add the beans and broccoli flowerets.

Spoon a layer of the bean and tomato mixture into the bottom of a greased ovenproof dish. Cover with a layer of sliced mozzarella cheese, then another layer of bean and tomato mixture. Continue with these layers until all the ingredients are used up, finishing with a layer of mozzarella.

Mix the shredded mozzarella and Parmesan together and sprinkle over the top of the cassserole. Bake in a preheated oven, 350°F, for 30-35 minutes. Serve hot, garnished with fresh herb sprigs, if you like.

Illustrated opposite

ZUCCHINI & TOMATO CHOUX PASTRY RING

Serves 3-4

¾ pound zucchini, trimmed and sliced

2 tablespoons corn oil

2 onions, chopped

1 sweet green pepper, cored, seeded and sliced

½ pound tomatoes, peeled and quartered

1 teaspoon dried oregano

2 teaspoons grated Parmesan cheese

salt and freshly ground black pepper

CHOUX PASTRY:

½ cup plus 2 tablespoons whole wheat flour

pinch of salt

½ stick butter

⅔ cup water

2 eggs, beaten

Place the zucchini slices in a colander, sprinkle with salt and set aside for 30 minutes to draw out some of the excess liquid.

Heat the corn oil in a large skillet, add the chopped onions and cook over a gentle heat for 5 minutes. Stir in the green pepper. Rinse and drain the zucchini and add them to the skillet. Cook for a further 5 minutes, stirring occasionally. Add the quartered tomatoes, oregano and seasoning to taste. Cook for about 10 minutes until beginning to soften. Set aside.

To make the choux paste, sift the flour and salt together on to a sheet of waxed paper, returning the bran retained in the sifter to the flour. Melt the butter in a small saucepan, add the measured water and bring to a boil. When bubbling, remove the pan from the heat and immediately add the flour all at once. Beat the mixture until it is smooth and leaves the sides of the pan clean. Let cool slightly, then gradually add the eggs, beating well between each addition.

Spoon the choux paste around the edge of a shallow 6-cup ovenproof dish. Spoon the vegetable mixture into the center and sprinkle with the grated Parmesan.

Cook in a preheated oven, 400°F, for 30-35 minutes until the choux pastry is golden brown and risen. Serve immediately with a green salad.

TOMATO RICE

Serves 4-6

½ stick butter
1 pound ripe tomatoes, peeled
and finely chopped
¼ teaspoon cayenne pepper
½ teaspoon sugar
1 large onion, sliced
1 tablespoon corn oil
½-inch piece of fresh ginger, peeled
and finely chopped
1 garlic clove, crushed
1⅔ cups long-grain rice, washed, soaked
in cold water for 30 minutes and drained
salt and freshly ground black pepper
chopped fresh parsley, for garnish

Melt half the butter in a saucepan. Add the tomatoes, cayenne, sugar and salt. Cook, stirring occasionally, for 5 minutes. Set aside.

Gently cook the onion in the corn oil and remaining butter in a large pan, stirring occasionally, for 3-4 minutes. Add the ginger and garlic and cook until the onion is soft. Add the rice, increase heat and cook, stirring, 1 minute. Pour in the tomato mixture, season, and add boiling water to cover rice by ½ inch. When the liquid boils rapidly, cover, reduce heat to very low and simmer 12-15 minutes or until rice is cooked and all the liquid has been absorbed. Serve immediately, garnished with chopped fresh parsley.

MACARONI WITH SAUSAGE & TOMATO SAUCE

Serves 4

1 pound Italian sausages, skinned
2 tablespoons olive oil
2 garlic cloves, crushed
1 onion, coarsely chopped
1 sweet red pepper, cored, seeded and
cut into cubes
1½ pounds beefsteak tomatoes,
peeled and chopped
1 teaspoon dried oregano
2 tablespoons tomato paste
6 tablespoons Marsala or sherry
½ pound macaroni
¼ stick butter
salt and freshly ground black pepper

Break each sausage into four or five pieces. Heat oil in a saucepan and cook garlic and onion until softened and colored. Add sausage to the pan; cook until browned. Add red pepper, tomatoes and oregano. Stir in tomato paste and Marsala or sherry with salt and pepper to taste. Cook gently, uncovered, for 12-15 minutes.

Cook macaroni in plenty of salted boiling water for 8-10 minutes, or follow package directions, until tender. Drain well, tip into a bowl and stir in the butter. Pour the sauce over the pasta, toss to mix, and serve.

SPAGHETTI WITH TOMATO & MUSSEL SAUCE

Serves 4

5 pints fresh mussels
⅔ cup water
⅓ cup olive oil
1 onion, finely chopped
2 garlic cloves, sliced
1½ pounds tomatoes, peeled and chopped
¾ pound spaghetti or vermicelli
salt and freshly ground black pepper
flat-leaf parsley, for garnish

First, prepare the mussels. Put them in a bowl or sink with cold water to cover. Discard any mussels which are open or which float to the top. Scrub the mussels to remove any barnacles and remove the beards. Soak in fresh cold water until ready to cook.

Put the mussels into a large saucepan with the measured water. Heat briskly, shaking the pan occasionally, for 5-6 minutes or until the shells open. Discard any mussels that do not open. Remove from the heat and drain off the water. Reserve a few of the mussels in their shells for the garnish. Remove the rest of the mussels from their shells and set aside.

Heat 3 tablespoons of the olive oil in a large saucepan. Add the chopped onion and sauté for 5 minutes until soft. Stir in the garlic, then add the chopped tomatoes. Simmer gently for about 30 minutes until the tomatoes have been reduced to a pulp.

Cook the spaghetti or vermicelli in a large saucepan of lightly salted boiling water for about 10 minutes, or according to package directions, until just tender. Drain the pasta thoroughly. Pour the remaining olive oil into a warm dish, add the pasta and toss until lightly coated.

Season the tomato sauce with salt and pepper to taste, add the shelled mussels and heat through, stirring. Pile the sauce on top of the pasta. Garnish with the reserved mussels and flat-leaf parsley and serve immediately.

Illustrated opposite

PASTA SHELLS
WITH RICH
TOMATO SAUCE

Serves 3-4

½ **pound whole wheat pasta shells**
or spaghetti

TOMATO SAUCE:

¼ **stick butter**
1 large onion, sliced
1 garlic clove, crushed
1½ **pounds ripe beefsteak tomatoes,**
peeled and chopped
2 tablespoons tomato paste
2 teaspoons sugar
2 tablespoons chopped fresh marjoram,
or 2 teaspoons dried oregano
⅔ **cup vegetable stock, or half stock**
and half red wine
salt and freshly ground black pepper

CRUNCHY DRESSING:

2 teaspoons butter
2 tablespoons sunflower seeds
½ **cup fresh whole wheat bread crumbs**

To make the tomato sauce, melt the butter in a large saucepan and sauté the onion and crushed garlic for about 5 minutes until tender but not brown. Add the chopped tomatoes, tomato paste, sugar, marjoram or oregano, and stock or stock and wine. Stir in salt and pepper to taste. Half cover the pan and

simmer gently for 25 minutes. Remove the lid, increase the heat and cook for 2-3 minutes more to reduce the sauce. It should have a thick, rich consistency. Keep the sauce hot.

Cook the pasta in a large pan of salted boiling water according to package directions, until just tender.

While the pasta is cooking, prepare the dressing. Heat the butter in a small skillet, add the sunflower seeds and brown slightly, stirring and shaking the pan (be careful as they will jump about in the heat), then stir in the bread crumbs. When both are brown, spoon onto a plate and set aside.

Drain the cooked pasta thoroughly and tip it into a warm serving dish, spoon the hot sauce over and top with the crunchy dressing. Serve immediately.

TOMATO & EGGPLANT SOUFFLE LASAGNE

Serves 4-6

2 eggplants, about 1 pound, cut into
½-inch thick slices
¼ cup corn oil
2 large onions, sliced
2 garlic cloves, crushed
5 ounces no pre-cook spinach lasagne
(*about 8 sheets*)
1½ pounds ripe tomatoes, sliced
1 tablespoon chopped fresh basil,
or 1 teaspoon dried
⅔ cup vegetable stock
salt and freshly ground black pepper

SOUFFLE TOPPING:

1 tablespoon butter
2 tablespoons all-purpose flour
1¼ cups milk
2 eggs, separated

Put the eggplant slices in a colander, sprinkle with salt and set aside for 30 minutes to draw out some of the excess liquid.

Heat 1 tablespoon of the oil in a large skillet. Sauté the onions and garlic for 5 minutes until soft but not brown. Spoon into a dish and set aside.

Rinse the eggplant slices, drain, then dry with paper towels. Heat 2 tablespoons of the remaining oil in the pan and cook half the slices on both sides until golden brown. Drain on paper towels. Add the rest of the oil to the pan and cook the remaining eggplant slices.

Lightly oil a large shallow ovenproof dish. Lay four lasagne sheets in the bottom. Cover with a layer of eggplant slices, then a layer of cooked onion, then a layer of tomato slices. Sprinkle with salt, plenty of black pepper and half the basil. Repeat the layering once more, using all the remaining lasagne, vegetables and herbs. Pour over the stock to enable the pasta to rehydrate.

To make the soufflé topping, melt the butter in a small saucepan, stir in the flour and cook for 1 minute. Gradually add the milk, stirring until the sauce boils and thickens. Cool slightly, then stir in the egg yolks and season.

Whisk the egg whites in a grease-free bowl until stiff and fold them carefully into the sauce. Spoon the mixture into the dish, covering the top layer completely. Bake in a preheated oven, 350°F, for 45 minutes until the soufflé has risen and is browned.

Serve the lasagne piping hot with bread to soak up the juices.

TOMATO PIZZA

Serves 1-2

1¾ cups bread flour
1 packet active yeast
6 tablespoons olive oil
1½ pounds tomatoes, peeled and chopped
1 onion, chopped
1 teaspoon sugar
1-2 garlic cloves, chopped
2 teaspoons dried oregano
2 sun-dried tomatoes, cut into thin strips
5 tablespoons freshly grated Parmesan cheese
salt and freshly ground black pepper

For the dough, sift flour into a bowl, stir in yeast. Make a well in the center, add ½ cup hand-hot water, 1 tablespoon of the oil and 1 teaspoon of salt. Mix to a soft dough, knead on lightly floured surface until smooth, about 10 minutes. Roll out to 10-inch circle. Place on a lightly floured baking sheet. Pinch a slightly thicker rim with your fingers. Cover with waxed paper, leave to rise for 30 minutes, while preparing topping.

In a skillet, cook the tomatoes, onion and sugar in 3 tablespoons of the oil over a low heat for 15 minutes, or until thick. Brush pizza base with a little of remaining oil, top with the sauce, then add the garlic, oregano, sun-dried tomatoes and salt and pepper. Sprinkle with cheese and remaining oil, bake in a preheated oven, 425°F, for 20-25 minutes until bubbling and golden. Serve hot.

TOMATO & MOZZARELLA PIZZA

Serves 1-2

3 tablespoons olive oil
1 pound Italian plum tomatoes,
peeled and chopped
1 homemade pizza base (*see opposite*)
⅔ cup shredded mozzarella cheese
½ cup sliced pepperoni
3 large tomatoes, sliced
5 sun-dried tomatoes, halved
1 sweet green pepper, sliced
freshly ground black pepper

Heat 2 tablespoons of the olive oil in a large skillet. Add the chopped plum tomatoes and cook over a low heat for 15 minutes, or until the sauce is thick.

Place the prepared pizza base on a lightly floured baking sheet. Spread the sauce over the pizza dough. Sprinkle over half of the mozzarella. Top with the pepperoni, sliced tomatoes, sun-dried tomatoes and green pepper. Sprinkle over the remaining cheese, olive oil and black pepper.

Bake in a preheated oven, 425°F, for 20-25 minutes until the pizza is bubbling and golden brown.

Illustrated opposite

TOMATO-STUFFED PANCAKES

Serves 4

BATTER:

1 cup all-purpose flour, sifted

¼ teaspoon salt

1 egg, beaten

1¼ cups milk

oil, for cooking

FILLING:

¼ stick butter

½ onion, finely chopped

4 tomatoes, peeled and coarsely chopped

1 cup chopped mushrooms

1 teaspoon mixed dried herbs

½ cup fresh white bread crumbs

salt and freshly ground black pepper

TOPPING:

3 tablespoons butter

6 tablespoons all-purpose flour

1¼ cups milk

¾ cup shredded Cheddar cheese

To make the pancake batter, sift the flour and salt together in a bowl. Make a well in the center and add the beaten egg and half of the milk. Gradually incorporate the flour into the liquid to make a smooth batter. Stir in the rest of the milk.

Grease an 8-inch skillet with a little of the oil. Pour in enough batter to cover the bottom of the pan, tilting the pan so that the batter covers it evenly. Cook over a moderate heat until the bottom of the pancake is golden brown, then flip or turn the pancake over and cook the other side briefly. Keep the pancake warm while making seven more pancakes in the same way.

For the filling, melt the butter and cook the chopped onion, tomatoes and mushrooms until reduced to a pulp. Stir in the herbs and bread crumbs, and season well. Divide the filling among the pancakes and roll them up. Arrange side by side in an ovenproof dish.

To make the sauce topping, melt the butter in a heavy-bottom saucepan. Stir in the flour and cook for 1 minute. Gradually add the milk, stirring until the sauce boils and thickens. Simmer for 3-4 minutes, stirring.

Stir ½ cup of the cheese into the white sauce, season and pour over the pancakes. Sprinkle over the remaining cheese. Bake in a preheated oven, 375°F, for 20 minutes.

TOMATO & BACON FONDUE

Serves 4

1 garlic clove
6 bacon slices
⅔ cup dry white wine
2 teaspoons cornstarch
2 beefsteak tomatoes, peeled
and finely chopped
1½ cups shredded Cheddar cheese
1½ cups shredded Swiss cheese
few drops of Worcestershire sauce
pinch of mustard powder
salt and freshly ground black pepper

Cut the garlic clove in half and rub the inside of a fondue pan with the cut edge. Discard the garlic. Cook the bacon until crisp, drain on paper towels, and chop into bite-size pieces.

Mix 1 tablespoon of wine with the cornstarch in a small bowl; pour remaining wine into fondue pan. Add tomatoes and heat gently until hot. Gradually stir in the cheeses, beating gently. Add the cornstarch mixture to the pan; stir over a moderate heat until thickened. Stir in the bacon. Add a few drops of Worcestershire sauce, a pinch of mustard powder and salt and pepper to taste.

Serve with cubes of crusty French bread, cauliflower flowerets and chunks of zucchini to dip into the fondue.

WALNUT, CHEESE & TOMATO LOAF

Serves 4-6

2 cups ground walnuts
½ pound tomatoes, peeled and thinly sliced
1 cup shredded Cheddar cheese or
Monterey Jack
1 onion, grated
1 tablespoon chopped fresh marjoram
or oregano
1 egg, beaten
salt and freshly ground black pepper

Combine the ground walnuts, sliced tomatoes, shredded cheese and onion and chopped herbs in a bowl. Add salt and pepper to taste and stir in the beaten egg.

Spoon the mixture into a lightly greased 7 x 3-inch loaf pan and press down well. Bake in a preheated oven, 400°F, for 30-40 minutes, or until brown on top. Cool the loaf in the pan, invert it on a serving platter and serve with a salad.

TOMATO & FETA TARTS

Makes 18-20

1½ pounds tomatoes, peeled,
seeded and chopped
1 small onion, finely chopped
2 garlic cloves, chopped
2 tablespoons tomato paste
1 tablespoon chopped fresh basil
2 teaspoons chopped fresh thyme
⅔ cup crumbled feta cheese
12 plump ripe olives, pitted
6 drained canned anchovy fillets,
split lengthwise
3 tablespoons olive oil
salt and freshly ground black pepper

DOUGH:

1 cup whole wheat flour
1 cup all-purpose flour
½ cup cream cheese, softened
generous pinch of salt
3 tablespoons plain yogurt
2 egg yolks

To make the dough, put the flours into a food processor with the cream cheese and process to a fine crumb texture. Beat the salt, yogurt and egg yolks together. Add to the dry ingredients and process until the mixture forms a ball of dough, being careful not to overmix. Wrap closely and chill for 1 hour before using.

Since this dough is more elastic than basic pie dough and is more prone to losing its shape, roll out the dough thinly on a floured board and then leave it to rest for 10 minutes before cutting. Using a fluted cutter stamp out circles from the dough and use to line 18-20 tart pans; press up the edges well.

Mix the chopped tomatoes, onion, garlic, tomato paste, basil and thyme in a shallow saucepan. Add salt and pepper to taste. Simmer for about 20 minutes until the mixture is thick and pulpy.

Divide the tomato filling among the tart cases, adding a little feta cheese to each one. Roll each ripe olive in a strip of anchovy fillet and place one on each tart. Dribble over a little olive oil.

Bake the tarts in a preheated oven, 375°F, for 25-30 minutes until the filling is a rich red color, and the pastry has taken on some of the color from the filling. Serve immediately.

Illustrated opposite

TOMATO PIE

Serves 4-6

1½ pounds ripe, firm tomatoes,
peeled and quartered
½ pound frozen puff pastry, thawed
¾ cup shredded Swiss or mild
Cheddar cheese
¼ stick butter, softened
¼ cup heavy cream
2 eggs, lightly beaten
salt and freshly ground black pepper

Squeeze tomato quarters gently over a colander to rid them of excess moisture. Chop and leave to drain in the colander.

Roll the pastry out thinly and line a 9-10-inch fluted pie pan. Sprinkle pastry evenly with ¼ cup of the cheese. Work remaining cheese in a bowl to a fluffy paste with the butter and cream. Then beat in the eggs and season lightly.

Season tomatoes and spread evenly over the pastry. Spoon the egg and cheese mixture over the tomatoes. Place pie on a preheated heavy baking sheet in a preheated oven, 425°F. After 15 minutes, reduce heat to 350°F. Bake pie for 20 minutes longer, or until filling is puffed and richly colored and pastry is crisp and cooked through. Serve the pie as an opener or with a salad as a main course.

TOMATO & BACON TURNOVERS

Makes 4

¼ stick butter
1 onion, finely chopped
6 ounces Canadian bacon, chopped
½ pound tomatoes, peeled,
seeded and chopped
1 tablespoon chopped fresh parsley
1 tablespoon tomato paste
½ pound frozen puff pastry, thawed
salt and freshly ground black pepper
beaten egg, to glaze

Melt butter in a skillet, add the onion and bacon and sauté, stirring, for 4 minutes. Add tomatoes, parsley and tomato paste with plenty of pepper to taste. Cook, stirring, for 5 minutes or until thickened. Set aside to cool.

On a floured board, roll out pastry to a 12-inch square. Cut into four equal squares and dampen the edges with egg. Divide the bacon filling among the squares. Fold over each square diagonally to form triangle-shaped turnovers. Press edges together to seal.

Brush turnovers with beaten egg and place on a greased baking sheet. Bake in a preheated oven, 425°F, for 25 minutes until golden. Cool on a wire rack.

TANDOORI CHICKEN IN TOMATO SAUCE

Serves 4

**3-pound broiler-fryer chicken, skinned
and cut into 8 pieces**
chopped fresh parsley, for garnish

MARINADE:

¼ cup lemon juice
1 garlic clove, crushed
½ teaspoon ground coriander
½ teaspoon chili powder
1 teaspoon garam masala
¼ cup plain yogurt
1 teaspoon ground cumin
1 tablespoon paprika
**1-inch piece of fresh ginger,
finely chopped**
2 tablespoons oil
salt and freshly ground black pepper

SAUCE:

½ stick butter
1 teaspoon salt
½ teaspoon sugar
1 pound tomatoes, peeled and quartered
1 teaspoon garam masala
3 tablespoons heavy cream

Make cuts all over the surface of the chicken. Mix the ingredients for the marinade in a bowl. Rub the mixture over the chicken pieces until well coated. Place the chicken on a plate, cover and leave in a cool place for 4 hours, or refrigerate overnight, to marinate.

Transfer the chicken portions to a greased roasting pan and baste with the oil. Cook in a preheated oven, 400°F, for 30 minutes. Baste with the juices several times during cooking.

To make the sauce, melt the butter in a large skillet and add the salt, sugar and tomatoes. Cook, uncovered, for about 15 minutes, stirring occasionally. Rub the mixture through a strainer or purée it first in a blender or food processor, and then rub through a strainer. Return the tomato sauce to the rinsed pan. Add the garam masala and simmer for 10 minutes. Remove the pan from the heat and stir in the cream.

Add the cooked chicken pieces to the sauce. Heat through but do not boil. Transfer to a heated serving dish, sprinkle with the chopped parsley and serve.

MICROWAVE METHOD: Marinade chicken as above. Place on a large roasting rack in a single layer. Place butter, salt, sugar and tomatoes in a casserole dish, cover and cook on High power for 7-8 minutes, stirring twice. Purée and strain. Add garam masala. Cook chicken on High for 7 minutes, then on Medium for 10-15 minutes or until juices run clear. Cover loosely. Reheat sauce on High for 3 minutes. Stir in cream and serve as above.

CHICKEN & TOMATO CURRY

Serves 4

½ stick butter
2 onions, finely chopped
1-inch piece of fresh ginger,
peeled and chopped
2 teaspoons garam masala
1 teaspoon ground cumin
¼ teaspoon cayenne pepper
⅔ cup plain yogurt
1 cup chopped tomatoes
3½-pound broiler-fryer chicken, cut into 8 pieces
⅔ cup chicken stock
salt

Melt the butter in a large saucepan, add the chopped onions and ginger and sauté over a gentle heat until soft. Add the garam masala, cumin and cayenne pepper and cook for 2 minutes, then gradually stir in the yogurt a tablespoon at a time. Stir in the chopped tomatoes with salt to taste and cook over a low heat for a further 2-3 minutes.

Add the chicken pieces and the stock to the saucepan. Bring to a boil, cover the pan and simmer the curry for 45 minutes or until the chicken is tender. Serve with rice pilaf.

COUNTRY CHICKEN WITH PEPPERS & TOMATOES

Serves 4

3-pound broiler-fryer chicken, cut into quarters,
or 4 chicken pieces
seasoned flour, for dredging
¼ cup corn oil
2 onions, chopped
2 sweet green peppers, cored, seeded and sliced
2 garlic cloves, crushed
1 pound plum tomatoes, chopped
2 cups red wine
1 tablespoon tomato paste
¾ cup chicken stock
1 teaspoon dried oregano
1 bay leaf
pitted ripe olives, for garnish

Coat the chicken pieces in the seasoned flour in a strong plastic bag. Shake off the excess flour. Heat the oil in a large skillet, add the onions and sauté for 3 minutes. Add the chicken and cook until golden all over.

Add all the remaining ingredients, except the ripe olives, to the pan. Cover and simmer gently for 40 minutes. Spoon the chicken and vegetables on to a warmed serving dish and garnish with the ripe olives. Serve at once.

Illustrated opposite

STEAK WITH FRESH TOMATO SAUCE

Serves 4

4 rib or rump steaks, ¾-inch thick
olive oil, for sprinkling and cooking
½ cup dry red wine or beef stock
salt and freshly ground black pepper
parsley sprigs, for garnish

SAUCE:

2 tablespoons olive oil
3 garlic cloves, crushed
1 pound plum tomatoes, peeled, seeded
and chopped
a few fresh basil leaves,
or ½ teaspoon dried oregano

Beat the steaks with a rolling pin to tenderize. Season, sprinkle with oil and leave to stand.

For the sauce, heat the oil in a saucepan, sauté the garlic for 1 minute. Add the tomatoes and season to taste. Bring to a boil then cook over a moderate heat for 5 minutes, until tomatoes are just softened. Add the basil or oregano.

Oil the base of a large skillet and sauté the steaks over a moderate heat for 2 minutes each side, until lightly browned. Add the wine or stock. Top each steak with a thick layer of the sauce, cover the pan tightly and cook over a low heat for 6-10 minutes or until the steaks are tender and cooked to your liking. Serve at once, garnished with parsley.

PORK CHOPS WITH JUNIPER BERRIES & TOMATOES

Serves 4

¼ cup olive oil
4 pork chops, about ½ pound each
2 shallots or small onions, chopped
1 garlic clove, chopped
8 juniper berries, coarsely crushed
2 cups chopped tomatoes,
⅓ cup gin or vodka
⅔ cup chicken stock
½ tablespoon chopped fresh thyme,
or ½ teaspoon dried
salt and freshly ground black pepper

Heat the oil in a deep skillet. Add the pork chops, cook briskly for 3-4 minutes each side to brown, then remove and keep warm. Add the shallots or onions to the pan, cook gently for about 2 minutes, then add the garlic and cook for a further minute.

Stir in the juniper berries and tomatoes, cook for 2-3 minutes, stirring. Then add the gin or vodka and boil rapidly over a brisk heat until reduced by half. Stir in the stock and the thyme. Seaon to taste with salt and pepper.

Return chops to pan, cover and simmer for 15-20 minutes, adding a little extra stock if necessary, until the chops are cooked through. Serve with baked potatoes and vegetables.

VEAL WITH TOMATOES

Serves 4

1½ pounds veal steak, about
½-inch thick, cut into 1-inch strips
1 tablespoon flour, for dusting
¼ cup olive oil
1 large onion, finely chopped
2 cups thinly sliced mushrooms
1 pound ripe tomatoes, peeled,
seeded and chopped
½ cup slivered almonds
2 garlic cloves, coarsely chopped
1 teaspoon ground cumin
1 tablespoon finely chopped fresh parsley
pinch of cayenne pepper
pinch of saffron
1 small fresh red chili, seeded and roughly
chopped, or 1 small dried red chili, seeded
and soaked in water for 5 minutes,
then drained and coarsely chopped
¼ cup water
salt and freshly ground black pepper

Season the strips of veal with salt and black pepper and dust with a little flour.

Pour half the olive oil into a large heavy-bottom skillet and heat. Add the finely chopped onion to the pan and cook for 2-3 minutes. Then add the sliced mushrooms and cook for 3-4 minutes. Remove the vegetables from the pan with a slotted spoon, place on a plate and set aside.

Add the remaining olive oil and sauté the strips of veal for 3 minutes each side, or until the veal is lightly browned. Remove from the skillet and set aside. Add the chopped tomatoes to the pan and simmer gently for 2-3 minutes.

Place the slivered almonds, coarsely chopped garlic, 1 teaspoon of salt, ground cumin, chopped parsley, cayenne, saffron and chopped chili in a blender or food processor with the water and process to a paste. Add this to the tomato mixture in the skillet and simmer for 5 minutes.

Stir in the veal, mushrooms and onions and simmer for 5 minutes until the veal is heated through. Serve with rice or boiled potatoes.

SHRIMP & TOMATO CURRY

Serves 3-4

1 pound raw jumbo shrimp peeled and deveined
salt, for sprinkling
½ stick butter or 4 tablespoons clarified butter
2 marmande tomatoes, peeled and sliced
3 onions, finely chopped
1 garlic clove, crushed
¼ teaspoon ground ginger
1 teaspoon chili powder
2 teaspoons ground coriander
½ teaspoon ground turmeric
2 tablespoons unsweetened shredded coconut
⅔ cup water
2 teaspoons garam masala

Sprinkle the shrimp lightly with salt. Heat the butter or clarified butter in a large skillet, add the shrimp and sauté over a moderate heat for 2 minutes. Push the shrimp to one side and stir in the tomatoes, onions, garlic and all the spices except the garam masala. Cook for 1 minute, then mix with the shrimp and cook for 4 minutes more.

Add the coconut and measured water to the pan and simmer for 5 minutes. Sprinkle on the garam masala and cook for 1 minute. Serve with plain boiled rice and a selection of side dishes.

CHILI SHRIMP & CHERRY TOMATOES

Serves 4

3 tablespoons corn oil
1 small onion, finely chopped
1-inch piece of fresh ginger,
peeled and finely chopped
2 garlic cloves, crushed
1-2 fresh chilies, seeded and chopped,
or 1-2 teaspoons chili powder
¾ pound raw Jumbo shrimp, peeled
with tails left on
6-8 cherry tomatoes, halved
2 tablespoons tomato paste
1 tablespoon red or white wine vinegar
pinch of sugar
½ teaspoon salt

Heat the oil in a wok or large skillet until hot. Add the onion, ginger, garlic and chilies or chili powder. Stir-fry for 2-3 minutes or until softened, taking care not to let the ingredients brown.

Add the shrimp, increase the heat to high, and stir-fry for 1-2 minutes, or until they turn pink. Add the remaining ingredients and stir-fry for several minutes or until the mixture is thick, taking care not to let the tomatoes lose their shape. Adjust the seasoning to taste and serve at once with noodles or rice.

Illustrated opposite

MEDITERRANEAN FISH & TOMATO CASSEROLE

Serves 4

3 bacon slices, chopped
1 large onion, finely chopped
1 garlic clove, crushed
1 small sweet green pepper, cored, seeded
and finely chopped
1 tablespoon all-purpose flour
⅔ cup dry white wine
⅔ cup water
2 beefsteak tomatoes, peeled,
seeded and chopped
½ teaspoon dried basil
1½ pounds firm white fish, skinned and cut into
large chunks
salt and freshly ground black pepper
chopped fresh parsley, for garnish

Heat bacon in a large heavy-bottom skillet until fat runs. Increase heat and cook the onion, garlic and green pepper for 5-6 minutes or until the onion is soft.

Stir in flour, cook for 1 minute. Gradually add wine and water, stirring constantly. Add tomatoes, basil and seasoning to taste. Bring sauce to a boil, stirring until it thickens. Add the fish. Cover, reduce heat and simmer for 10-15 minutes or until cooked. Serve garnished with parsley.

FRESH TUNA WITH TOMATOES

Serves 4

4 tuna steaks
flour, for dusting
3 tablespoons olive oil
1 small onion, chopped
1 garlic clove, crushed
1½ pounds marmande tomatoes,
peeled and chopped
2 tablespoons chopped fresh parsley
1 bay leaf
4 anchovy fillets, mashed
6 pitted ripe olives
salt and freshly ground black pepper

Season the tuna with salt and pepper and dust with flour. Heat half the oil in a large shallow skillet. Sauté the fish quickly until golden on both sides. Carefully transfer to a plate.

Add the remaining oil to the pan. When hot, add the onion and garlic and sauté for 5 minutes until soft. Stir in the tomatoes, parsley, bay leaf and anchovies. Bring to a boil and cook for about 10 minutes, or until the mixture has reduced to a thin sauce.

Season with pepper, return the fish to the pan and simmer gently for 15 minutes, turning once. Turn off the heat, add the olives and leave for 5 minutes. Transfer to a warm serving dish and serve immediately.

TOMATO BREAD

Makes 2 loaves

4-5 sun-dried tomatoes, minced
6 cups bread flour
1 teaspoon salt
1 teaspoon sugar
¼ stick butter or margarine,
or 1 tablespoon olive or corn oil
1 cake (⅗ *ounce*) compressed yeast,
or 1 package rapid-rise active yeast

Place the sun-dried tomatoes in a small bowl. Add enough boiling water to cover and set aside for 2-3 minutes.

Sift the flour and salt into a large bowl and stir in the sugar. Cut in the fat or add the oil. If using compressed yeast, put it into a separate bowl. If using rapid-rise dry yeast, add it to the flour in the bowl.

Drain the sun-dried tomatoes, reserving the soaking liquid in a liquid measure. Make it up to 2 cups with lukewarm water. The temperature of the liquid should be about 110°F. Cream the compressed yeast, add the liquid, top with a sprinkling of flour and leave for about 10 minutes, or until the surface is covered with bubbles. Blend with the flour. If using rapid-rise dry yeast, stir the liquid into the yeast and flour and blend to a dough.

Tip the dough out on to a lightly floured surface and knead thoroughly until the dough is firm and elastic and no longer feels sticky. Knead in the chopped tomatoes.

Return the dough to the mixing bowl and cover the bowl with plastic wrap. Leave in a warm place for about 1 hour or until the dough has doubled in bulk. Punch down the dough and shape.

To make two loaves: grease and warm two 7 x 3-inch loaf pans. Divide the dough in half. Press out each half to a neat rectangle, the same length and three times the width of each pan. Fold the dough to fit the pans and place in the pans with the fold underneath.

To make two split-crust loaves: form the dough into two large sausage shapes and place on lightly greased baking sheets. Make equally spaced shallow cuts along the top of each.

Cover the dough lightly and leave until nearly doubled in bulk. This takes at least 20 minutes.

Bake the loaves in a preheated oven, 425°F, for about 35 minutes or until cooked. When cooked the loaves should sound hollow when rapped on the bottom. Remove the loaves from the pans, if using. If the sides are not as crusty as you like, simply place on a flat baking sheet and return to the oven for a few minutes.

Illustrated on pages 2-3

SALSA

Makes about 4 pounds

2 pounds ripe tomatoes, peeled and chopped
2 pounds sweet red peppers, cored, seeded
and finely chopped
1 pound onions, finely chopped
2 red chilies, seeded and finely chopped
2 cups red wine vinegar
1 cup firmly packed light brown sugar
4 tablespoons mustard seeds
2 tablespoons celery seeds
1 tablespoon paprika
2 teaspoons salt
2 teaspoons pepper

Combine all the ingredients in a large saucepan. Bring to a boil over a moderate heat, then lower the heat and simmer, uncovered, for about 30 minutes until most of the liquid has evaporated and the relish is of a thick, pulpy consistency. Stir the mixture frequently.

Sterilize three 1 pound jars. Put the clean jars open end up on a baking sheet and place in a preheated oven, 275°F, for about 10 minutes until hot. Put the relish into the hot jars. When cool, seal with vinegar-proof covers. Label the jars and store in a cool, dry place. Refrigerate once opened.

All jellies, jams and preserves should be processed in a boiling water-bath canner according to the U.S.D.A. guidelines.

GREEN TOMATO & APPLE CHUTNEY

Makes about 4 pounds

1 pound cooking apples, peeled,
cored and coarsely chopped
2 pounds green tomatoes, chopped
1 pound onions, chopped
2 garlic cloves, crushed
2 green chilies, seeded and chopped
1 teaspoon ground ginger
1 teaspoon salt
½ teaspoon turmeric
¼ teaspoon ground cloves
⅓ cup golden raisins
1¼ cups vinegar
1⅓ cups firmly packed dark brown sugar

Combine all the ingredients in a large pan. Bring to a boil, stirring occasionally, reduce heat and simmer, uncovered, for 1¼-1½ hours, until excess liquid has evaporated and chutney is thick. Stir occasionally to make sure that the chutney does not stick to the bottom of the pan. Have ready warmed pots. Spoon in the hot chutney and top with small rounds of waxed paper, waxed sides down. Cover with airtight lids while hot. Label and store, unopened, for at least 1 month to mature. Unopened jars may be stored for up to 6 months in a cool, dry place.

Illustrated opposite

BASIC TOMATO SAUCE

Makes about 4 cups

2 mild onions, finely chopped
3 tablespoons olive oil
4 plump garlic cloves, peeled but left whole
½ large sweet green pepper, cored, seeded
and finely diced
1 large celery stalk, finely diced
3 pounds ripe tomatoes, peeled,
and coarsely chopped
1 bay leaf
2 teaspoons dried oregano or marjoram
1 teaspoon dried basil
1 teaspoon sugar (*optional*)
salt and freshly ground black pepper

Gently cook the onions in the oil in a large saucepan until soft. Add whole garlic cloves, and when lightly colored, add the pepper and celery. Cook gently, stirring occasionally, until the vegetables have softened.

Add the tomatoes and herbs, seasoning lightly. Bring sauce slowly to simmering point, cover and cook gently, stirring occasionally and mashing the tomatoes with the back of a spoon, for 40-45 minutes, or until sauce is thick and richly flavored. Adjust the seasoning, adding sugar if necessary. Remove and discard the garlic before serving the sauce with broiled sausage links or chicken drumsticks, as a pasta sauce or as a topping for pizza.

FIVE-MINUTE TOMATO SAUCE

Serves 4-6

1 pound ripe beefsteak tomatoes,
peeled and quartered
a few scallions
2-3 basil leaves, or pinch of dried
1 teaspoon brown sugar
2 tablespoons tomato paste
salt and freshly ground black pepper

Place all the ingredients in a blender or food processor and blend to a purée. Tip into a saucepan and heat for a few minutes.

This thin sauce has the fresh flavor of uncooked tomatoes. It is important to use scallions as the flavor of onion is too harsh for this short cooking time.

MICROWAVE METHOD: Prepare sauce as above. Place in a jug or bowl, cover loosely and cook on High for 3 minutes, stirring twice during cooking.

TOMATO MAYONNAISE

Makes about 2 cups

½ pound ripe tomatoes, peeled,
seeded and diced
2 teaspoons tomato paste
1 tablespoon chopped fresh basil
salt and freshly ground black pepper

MAYONNAISE:

2 egg yolks
2 teaspoons Dijon mustard
1¼ cups olive oil, or half and half olive and
corn oil
1 tablespoon white wine vinegar

To make the mayonnaise, beat the egg yolks and mustard in a bowl, and add the oil, drop by drop, beating constantly. As it starts to thicken, add oil in a steady stream, then stir in the vinegar with salt and pepper to taste. Alternatively, place the egg yolks, mustard and 1 tablespoon of the oil in a blender or food processor and process for 5 seconds. Dribble the remaining oil through the feed tube with the motor running, until it is all amalgamated. Add the vinegar, with salt and pepper to taste and process for about 3 seconds more.

Mix the tomatoes, tomato paste and basil in a bowl. Stir in 1 tablespoon of the mayonnaise and mix well. Fold in the remaining mayonnaise. Adjust seasoning to taste.

PISTOU

Makes about ⅔ cup

1 large ripe tomato, cut in half horizontally
1 cup chopped fresh basil
¼ cup chopped pignoli (*pine nuts*)
2 garlic cloves, crushed
¼ cup grated Parmesan cheese
¼ cup olive oil

Broil the tomato until soft and quite blackened on the surface. Remove the skin, chop the flesh and set aside.

Put the chopped basil in a mortar and pound until crushed. Add the pignoli and garlic and pound again. Add the chopped tomato. Continue to pound the mixture, adding the Parmesan until smooth.

Pour on the oil, drop by drop, as if making mayonnaise, continuing to pound constantly. The sauce should have the consistency of creamed butter. Serve with whole wheat spaghetti, tagliatelle, gnocchi, noodles, or in a minestrone-type soup.

SPICY TOMATO DIP

Serves 8

2 tablespoons corn oil
1 large onion, finely chopped
2 large garlic cloves, finely chopped
1 pound tomatoes, quartered
2 tablespoons wine vinegar
1 tablespoon sugar
½ teaspoon ground ginger
cayenne pepper, to taste
½ teaspoon paprika
½ teaspoon salt

Heat the oil in a saucepan. Add the onion and garlic and cook gently, stirring occasionally, for 10 minutes. Do not let the onion brown.

Add the tomatoes, vinegar, sugar and ground ginger, with cayenne to taste. Stir. Simmer the mixture, partially covered, for 35-40 minutes until thick and pulpy, stirring occasionally toward the end of the cooking time.

Purée the dip in a blender or food processor, or rub through a strainer into a bowl. Cool.

Add the paprika and salt before storing or serving the dip. It will keep, covered, in the refrigerator for 4-5 days and is delicious served with broiled sausage links.

TOMATO AND CHILI DIP

Makes 1 pound

3 tablespoons peanut oil
2 garlic cloves, crushed
**1 small piece of tamarind, crushed,
or ¼ cup lime juice**
1 small onion, finely chopped
**3 green or red chilies, seeded and
cut into fine strips**
1 pound firm tomatoes, peeled and diced
1 tablespoon dark brown sugar
⅓ cup canned coconut milk
1 tablespoon tomato paste
salt

FOR GARNISH:

cilantro sprigs
finely chopped green chili

Heat oil in a small skillet, add garlic, tamarind or lime juice and onion, and stir-fry for 1 minute. Add chilies and tomatoes and stir-fry for a few minutes. Add sugar and season with salt. Stir in coconut milk and tomato purée.

Bring to a boil, reduce the heat and cook for 10-15 minutes, until the mixture is fairly dry. Let cool, cover and chill until required. Serve garnished with cilantro and green chili. (It will keep in the refrigerator for about a week.)

Illustrated opposite

TOMATO MARMALADE

Makes about 3 pounds

**3 pounds ripe tomatoes, peeled and
coarsely chopped**
2 small oranges, thinly sliced and quartered
1 lemon, thinly sliced and halved
5 cups sugar

Place a sieve over a small bowl and seed the
tomatoes, placing seeds into the sieve and
reserve the juice. Place the tomatoes in a large
heavy-bottom saucepan with the juice. Add
the orange and lemon slices to the tomatoes
and simmer uncovered for 30 minutes. Add
the sugar and stir until dissolved. Bring to a
boil and boil for about 1 hour or until setting
point is reached: put a little marmalade on a
very cold saucer; let cool. As it cools, if the
setting point is reached a skin will form on the
surface and will wrinkle when the marmalade
is gently pushed with one finger. Alternatively,
use a candy thermometer – this should register
220°F when setting point is reached.

Sterilize three 1 pound jars, following the
directions in the recipe for Salsa on page 56.

Pour the marmalade into the hot jars. Top
with small rounds of waxed paper waxed sides
down. Cover with airtight lids when cold.
Label and store the marmalade in a cool,
dry place.

CARROT & TOMATO JUICE

Makes about 2 ½ cups

1 pound carrots, thinly sliced
1 pound tomatoes, quartered
¼ cup lemon juice
juice of 2 oranges
⅔ cup plain yogurt
1 teaspoon sugar
few drops of Tabasco sauce

Place the carrots, tomatoes, lemon and
orange juice in a blender or food processor
and work to a purée. Rub through a strainer
to remove the seeds. Stir in the sugar,
Tabasco and yogurt. Serve immediately, or
chill for 1 hour first.

HOMEMADE
TOMATO JUICE

A glut of tomatoes provides the perfect opportunity for a supply of delicious, fresh, concentrated juice for the winter. Cocktails, clear consommés, soups and sauces can be made at a moment's notice. Just be sure to store the jars in a dark cupboard, since strong light tends to fade the brilliant color of the juice.

Rinse the tomatoes. Chop them up if they are large and pack them into a heavy-bottom saucepan. Add a sprinkling of salt and sugar, but no water. Put the pan over the lowest possible heat and cook very slowly, uncovered, stirring and mashing occasionally with a wooden spoon or pestle. When the liquid comes to simmering point, continue to cook gently until the tomatoes are quite soft. Continue simmering until some of the excess water has evaporated.

Purée the tomatoes and the juice through a food processor, discarding the seeds and skins. If the tomatoes are a very "seedy" variety, it is wise to push them through a coarse strainer first; too many seeds puréed into the juice can give it a bitter flavor. For the same reason, a blender should not be used without this preliminary straining since it tends to do too efficient a job on skins and seeds.

Pour the juice back into the pan and let it simmer, uncovered, stirring occasionally, until it has thickened to a rich, creamy consistency.

Meanwhile, prepare glass canning jars for the juice. Wash them, rinse out with boiling water and drain upside down on a rack, then keep warm in the oven.

Prepare a double thickness of corrugated cardboard, or use a thick cloth, to line the bottom of a preserving kettle or pan large enough to take the jars closely side by side.

Season the concentrated tomato juice to taste with more salt, sugar and freshly ground black pepper. A leaf or two of fresh basil pushed into some of the jars will make a delightful variation. Quickly pour the hot juice into the jars as the pulp deteriorates if left exposed to the air. Seal, but not too tightly.

Arrange the jars in the pan. Pour boiling water over the jars to totally cover. Then slowly let the water come back to a boil and maintain at 210°F for 15 minutes to sterilize the juice.

As soon as the jars can be handled, lift them out of the pan. Set the jars aside to rest for 2-3 minutes before securing the tops as tightly as possible.

The following day, test the seal. Remove the screwbands or clips. Lift each jar by its lid. If properly sealed the lid will stay on securely and the juice may be kept for up to 6 months. If the jar has not been sealed properly, put in the refrigerator and use within 4-5 days or re-process the juice.